Discover Your Inner Treasure™

(Inspired by Courage in our Hearts™ ~ A Family's Love Story)

Alex, Raz, Larry and Charisma Stephen

ISBN-10: 099107971X
ISBN-13: 978-0-9910797-1-1

INTRODUCTION

Discover Your Inner Treasure™ is the accompaniment to and was inspired by our book, **Courage in our Hearts™**
~ A Family's Love Story.

We encourage you to read the story of our journey from Trinidad to the United States in search of a bright future for our son and, ultimately, for our entire family. Once you read **Courage in our Hearts™**, please read through this book's ten modules, which correspond with the chapters in **Courage**, and complete the exercises. By implementing the strategies, lessons and steps we offer, you are sure to see transformation in various areas of your life.

Also by Alex and Raz Stephen:

- Courage in our Hearts™
~A Family's Love Story

- Transformation/Lifestyle Coaching

-www.NextLevelRiches.com (Training System)

-www.MeetwithAlex.com   (Transformation Coaching)

-Inspirational Life Quotes...A Collection for your Daily Motivation

-How to Care for Orchids: For Busy People

-How to Have the Best Individual Education Plan (IEP) Goals: For Your Child's Education

CONTENTS

DEDICATION

This book is dedicated to Mr. Imran Farook Mohamed, Raz's dad. A great role model who was dedicated to the Divine, his family, his noble teaching profession and his community. Education was his passion. It is an honor to see his qualities in our children and grandchildren.

"When the student is ready, the teacher will appear." ~Lao Tzu

Alex, Raz, Larry and Charisma Stephen
December 19, 2013

Chapter 1

THE LOVE MODULE

"To a child, love is spelled t.i.m.e."
~Unknown~

WORKSHEETS

Love is powerful. Love is one of the greatest and long-lasting forces in the universe. Love is the ultimate problem solver. Love heals and strengthens your self-love. Love can make you whole by piecing together the parts of your self-image that may be broken from past negative influences.

I.   Think about a time you felt an overwhelming urge to love yourself or others. How did you feel? Did you allow yourself to feel what you were feeling? Did you readily embrace what you were feeling? Did you allow your feelings to manifest? How did you feel once you allowed yourself to do something loving for yourself and others?

Write your responses in the space provided. Don't worry about proofreading. Write to reveal what is inside, not to be a critic of your writing. Free write.

Success is a journey, not a destination. The road will not always be easy. In life, love allows you to enjoy the good times and develop the strength to handle the challenges, which are sure to come. We grew closer through the fun times and the rough spots. We recognize that spending over forty years together is a great achievement. You can accomplish it, too. However, remember that it does not have to be perfect.

II.   What is your definition of success? Write about a time when you felt successful. What happened before success arrived? How did you monitor your progress along the way? Who or what inspired you? How did you reward yourself once you met your goal(s)?

_____
_____
_____
_____
_____
_____
_____
_____
_____
_____
_____
_____
_____
_____
_____
_____
_____
_____
_____
_____
_____
_____
_____
_____
_____
_____
_____
_____
_____

ALEX, RAZ, LARRY AND CHARISMA STEPHEN

Review the gems of "The Circle of Love."

III.   Think about a relationship that means a great deal to you. Ponder a relationship that you would like to see change for the best. Write about one of the relationships. How will you change yourself to change your relationships?   Choose one concept from the list below, and write about how it can help you strengthen your relationship.

"The Circle of Love"

1. Love is the greatest gift you can give and receive.
2. "The Circle of Love" starts with you loving yourself, and then you loving others, which is returned to you multiplied, strengthening your love for yourself.
3. Practice the golden rule: Do unto others as you will have them do unto you.
4. The simple things mean the most.
5. Show respect for the values of others.
6. Forgive so that you will be forgiven.
7. Work as a team.
8. Sometimes you need to compromise for the good of the team.
9. Agree to disagree.
10. Celebrate victories, small and large.
11. Practice open communication.
12. Be courteous.
13. Be mature and apologize.
14. Be grateful for the kindness shown by your partner, children and life.

_____
_____
_____
_____
_____
_____
_____

ALEX, RAZ, LARRY AND CHARISMA STEPHEN

_____
_____
_____
_____
_____
_____
_____
_____
_____
_____
_____
_____
_____
_____
_____
_____
_____
_____
_____
_____
_____
_____
_____
_____
_____
_____
_____
_____
_____
_____
_____
_____
_____
_____
_____
_____
_____
_____
_____

Chapter 2

THE ACCEPTANCE MODULE

"Understanding is the first step to acceptance, and only with acceptance can there be recovery."
~J.K. Rowling~

WORKSHEETS

Whenever life gets complicated, acceptance is a critical step to accurately assess the situation and determine how to proceed. Acceptance is a process, and at times it can be difficult to do. For many of us, where we are and what we are facing is the exact opposite of what we would like in our lives. But it is impossible to create a plan for moving forward if you are not willing to accept where you are. You must acknowledge all facts. When you release the resistance and the angst and allow things to be, you open the space for options, avenues and blessings to occur.

I.   Think about a time when you failed to accept one of the circumstances of your life. Describe the stress you experienced as a result of your non-acceptance. Then think of how you moved beyond the obstacle of non-acceptance. Who helped you in the process? How did you finally reach a healing place of acceptance?

_____

_____

Non-acceptance closes the door to opportunities.

II.   Think of a recent challenge of non-acceptance in your life. Ask yourself the following question: What can I do to move into total acceptance?   What research can you do to support you in gaining acceptance?   Make a list of the people who have overcome similar challenges. Explain below how you will tie your goals to what is important to you. Describe your triumphant future.

_____

_____

_____

_____

_____

_____

_____

_____

_____

_____

_____

_____

_____

_____

_____

_____

_____

_____

_____

_____

_____

_____

_____

_____

_____

_____

_____

_____

_____

_____

_____

_____

_____

ALEX, RAZ, LARRY AND CHARISMA STEPHEN

III.   If you are facing a serious health challenge, what is your vision for a perfect   solution? Using what you have learned from reading about the Stephen Family's love story, write a paragraph about how you would proceed proactively.

_____

_____

_____

_____

_____

_____

_____

_____

_____

_____

_____

_____

_____

_____

_____

_____

_____

_____

_____

_____

_____

_____

_____

_____

_____

_____

_____

_____

_____

_____

_____

_____

_____

_____

_____

_____

_____

_____

_____

Chapter 3

THE FAMILY MODULE

"It's all about the power of unconditional love; it is great to be able to give and receive it."
~Charisma Stephen~

WORKSHEETS

Family Jewels exist in every family. Take a quiet moment to mine the jewels in your family.

I.   Think of 3 role models in your family, and make a list of the reasons why these family members are blessings to you. How will you invite them to support you in your endeavors?

FAMILY JEWELS

1. Great role models exist in your immediate and extended family. Identify and utilize these role models.
2. Appreciate and utilize extended family support.
3. Thankfulness teaches gratitude, love, humility and appreciation

for what you have, instead of what's missing.
4.   Enjoy the power of unconditional love.
5.   In a family, love can be spelled in various ways: acceptance, communication and appreciation.

_____
_____
_____
_____
_____
_____
_____
_____
_____
_____
_____
_____
_____
_____
_____
_____
_____
_____
_____
_____
_____
_____
_____
_____
_____
_____
_____
_____
_____
_____
_____
_____

Recently, my family and I went to a T. Harv Eker seminar together. Everyone I met was so amazed that we were doing this as a family. To me, it just made sense. We started this journey together, why not continue it together. If we are going to continue growing and continue being success-minded, we must do so as a family, not only as individuals. What good is a blessing if you cannot share it with those you love?

II.   Plan an event in which several members of your family enjoy a special gala. What would this event look like? Which family members would you invite and why? Be sure to indicate if your planned gala is an educational, spiritual or social event. Include its location and the culminating family debriefing afterwards.

_____
_____
_____
_____
_____
_____
_____
_____
_____
_____
_____
_____
_____
_____
_____
_____
_____
_____
_____
_____
_____
_____
_____
_____
_____
_____
_____

III.   Think of a time when you practiced unconditional love towards a family member. Describe the experience, and explain the affect the experience had on you and the family member.

_____
_____
_____
_____
_____
_____
_____
_____
_____
_____
_____
_____
_____
_____
_____
_____
_____
_____
_____
_____
_____
_____
_____
_____
_____
_____
_____
_____
_____
_____
_____
_____
_____
_____
_____
_____

Chapter 4

THE MISSION MODULE

"Get on a Mission to live your Passion!"
~Alex Stephen~

WORKSHEETS

There is no magic in small dreams. The magic is in dreaming big and believing in your ability to achieve your goals. Never fear failing. Failure is only feedback about what does not work.

I.   Paint a portrait in words of your dreams. What do you dream about? How long have you nurtured your dreams? Do you ever fear not being able to achieve your dreams? Do you have role models who have already achieved something similar to your dreams? Have you taken the first step towards the journey of your dreams?

_____
_____
_____
_____
_____
_____
_____

ALEX, RAZ, LARRY AND CHARISMA STEPHEN

Goal setting is a powerful tool that can motivate you into making your WHY a reality. As you set and achieve your goals, you will build your self-confidence.

II.   Start by listing your goals, using empowering language in the present tense, instead of the future tense, with specific dates, times and measurable items. For example, "I have the outline for my book for review at the end of the month now." Precision is the key. List 3 goals for yourself in each of these goal-making categories: Personal, Career/Business, Giving Back and Spiritual.

_____
_____
_____
_____
_____
_____
_____
_____
_____
_____
_____
_____
_____
_____
_____
_____
_____
_____
_____
_____
_____
_____
_____
_____
_____
_____
_____
_____

ALEX, RAZ, LARRY AND CHARISMA STEPHEN

It is common for parents to want their children to be independent. We wanted both our children to have a bright future. We wanted them to be happy and successful. And in our minds, education was the path that would pave the way for them.

III.   What do you see as the path for your children to have a good life?

_____

_____

_____

_____

_____

_____

_____

_____

_____

_____

_____

_____

_____

_____

_____

_____

_____

_____

_____

_____

_____

_____

_____

_____

_____

_____

_____

_____

_____

_____

_____

_____

_____

_____

_____

_____

_____

Chapter 5

THE COMMUNICATION MODULE

"The single biggest problem in communication is the illusion that it has
taken place."
~George Bernard Shaw~

WORKSHEETS

We often forget that the whole purpose of communication is for
spirits to commune. To commune in this sense means to converse
together with sympathy and confidence, to interchange sentiments or
feelings, and to take counsel. In all relationships, there is a higher
order than the individuals involved.

I.   What does communication look like in your family? Would
you say it is effective? What would you like to change about the way
your family communicates? What would you maintain? How
important is communication to you?

_____
_____
_____
_____
_____

ALEX, RAZ, LARRY AND CHARISMA STEPHEN

Where there is resistance, things slow down, and when there is no resistance, abundance is manifested. When we communicate with an unselfish love that says, "I wish for you, what I wish for myself; therefore, I am on board," it helps to resolve conflict and eliminate resistance.

II.   Identify a time in your life when you thrived in a relationship based on non-resistant communication. What did this relationship look like? Explain how it was effective.

_____
_____
_____
_____
_____
_____
_____
_____
_____
_____
_____
_____
_____
_____
_____
_____
_____
_____
_____
_____
_____
_____
_____
_____
_____
_____
_____
_____

Think about how you communicate, especially within your family. Look for areas where you can improve your communication with your spouse, children, parents, siblings, colleagues and friends. Obstacles and challenges should not deter you from communicating with your loved ones and others; they should have the opposite effect, which is to create opportunities for more communication.

III.   Think of 2 groups from the list above and identify ways in which you can become a better communicator. Describe the group and explain how you are going to bring about a shift in the way you communicate. How will you practice non-resistant communication?

_____
_____
_____
_____
_____
_____
_____
_____
_____
_____
_____
_____
_____
_____
_____
_____
_____
_____
_____
_____
_____
_____
_____
_____
_____
_____
_____
_____

ALEX, RAZ, LARRY AND CHARISMA STEPHEN

Chapter 6

THE PASSION MODULE

"Passion is energy. Feel the power that comes from focusing on what
excites you."
~Oprah Winfrey~

WORKSHEETS

As you pursue your goals, there will be times when the challenges
seem insurmountable. This may be a sign that you are close to the
finish line. You must follow your passion, even if the path is filled
with obstacles.

I.   Write about the obstacles that seemingly hinder you from
reaching your goals. How do you respond to them? Have you
always responded to them in a positive way? If not, how did you
respond to them? Explain.

_____
_____
_____
_____
_____
_____

ALEX, RAZ, LARRY AND CHARISMA STEPHEN

Use your passion to create new paths. When you follow your passion with commitment, obstacles move out of your way.

II.   In following your passion, have you ever allowed it to create new paths for you? Have you been following your passion with commitment and a sense of urgency? If not, why not?

_____

_____

_____

_____

_____

_____

_____

_____

_____

_____

_____

_____

_____

_____

_____

_____

_____

_____

_____

_____

_____

_____

_____

_____

_____

_____

_____

_____

_____

_____

_____

_____

_____

_____

_____

_____

ALEX, RAZ, LARRY AND CHARISMA STEPHEN

Many settle before achieving their goals. You should always prepare the path you desire for yourself.

III.   Have you ever found yourself settling on achieving your goals? Describe what it felt like to settle. Identify 3 recourses you might have taken in place of settling.

_____
_____
_____
_____
_____
_____
_____
_____
_____
_____
_____
_____
_____
_____
_____
_____
_____
_____
_____
_____
_____
_____
_____
_____
_____
_____
_____
_____
_____
_____
_____
_____
_____
_____
_____

ALEX, RAZ, LARRY AND CHARISMA STEPHEN

Chapter 7

THE CONFIDENCE MODULE

"We gain strength, and courage, and confidence by each experience in
which we really stop to look fear in the face...we must do that which we
think we cannot."
~Eleanor Roosevelt~

WORKSHEETS

Most of us admire self-confident people, as confidence is important
in all areas of life. It helps you to be successful, and when you are,
people are inspired. Your confidence shows up in your behavior, in
the way you speak and in the words you choose. When you are
confident, you accept tough challenges and remain persistent.

I.   Think of a time when you were self-confident. What
happened? How were you successful? Did your behavior inspire
others? What challenges did you overcome while being confident?

_____
_____
_____
_____
_____

ALEX, RAZ, LARRY AND CHARISMA STEPHEN

Confidence can be learned. Doing so requires a shift in mindset. We begin by believing in our ability to achieve our goals and dreams. We use focus and determination to move us forward. Make the commitment to grow your confidence.

II.   Reflect on your successes, achievements and strengths. Describe self-confident role models and mentors in your life. How can you learn from their experiences?

_____
_____
_____
_____
_____
_____
_____
_____
_____
_____
_____
_____
_____
_____
_____
_____
_____
_____
_____
_____
_____
_____
_____
_____
_____
_____
_____
_____

ALEX, RAZ, LARRY AND CHARISMA STEPHEN

Many times, opportunities are disguised as challenges.

III.   Write about a time in your life when an opportunity came to you disguised as a challenge. How did you meet the challenge? What opportunity did the challenge present?

_____

_____

_____

_____

_____

_____

_____

_____

_____

_____

_____

_____

_____

_____

_____

_____

_____

_____

_____

_____

_____

_____

_____

_____

_____

_____

_____

_____

_____

_____

_____

_____

_____

_____

_____

_____

_____

_____

_____

_____

Chapter 8

THE PERSEVERANCE MODULE

"Do not pray for fewer challenges; pray for more wisdom."
~Raz Stephen~

WORKSHEETS

In order to stay confident and persevere, you may wish to join or create a mastermind group. A mastermind group is a powerful and often effective tool for generating ideas and moving forward with your goals. The group consists of two or more minds with a shared commitment. You work in harmony with others and provide support, solutions and referrals in a non-threatening atmosphere. This group can help you stay motivated and positive. An effective mastermind group allows you to draw ideas and opinions from the collective wisdom of each member. It also creates accountability.

I.   Pretend you have organized a mastermind group. Who are the members of the group? Why did you select them to support you on a particular goal? What goal(s) does the group have in common? Think of 2 ways to be accountable to one another.

_____

_____

ALEX, RAZ, LARRY AND CHARISMA STEPHEN

As you strive towards your specific results, you will start to experience some form of fear: fear of success, fear of failure, or fear of criticism. Sometimes fear is like an anchor; it can weigh you down and drown you, if you are not careful.

II.   Think of a mantra to impress on your subconscious mind that allows you to break fear's crippling hold. Write it, and capitalize the words that would be emphasized. Practice reciting the mantra whenever you feel fear. Have fun.

_____

_____

_____

_____

_____

_____

_____

_____

_____

_____

_____

_____

_____

_____

_____

_____

_____

_____

_____

_____

_____

_____

_____

_____

_____

_____

_____

_____

_____

_____

_____

_____

_____

ALEX, RAZ, LARRY AND CHARISMA STEPHEN

Faith has no limits. Jeremiah 29:11 says, "For I know the plans I have for you, says the Lord, plans for welfare and not for evil, to give you a future and a hope." When we expect miracles in our lives, we see them made manifest every day. Life itself is a miracle.

III.   Quietly reflect on your day, week, month or year. Ponder the everyday miracles that exist in your life. Think of the extraordinary ones. Write about 3 miracles in your life.

_____
_____
_____
_____
_____
_____
_____
_____
_____
_____
_____
_____
_____
_____
_____
_____
_____
_____
_____
_____
_____
_____
_____
_____
_____
_____
_____
_____
_____
_____

Chapter 9

THE GRATITUDE MODULE

"Feeling gratitude and not expressing it is like wrapping a present and not
giving it."
~William Arthur Ward~

WORKSHEETS

A feeling of warmth may overcome us when someone expresses
sincere gratitude for something that we have done. We often get that
same feeling when we acknowledge someone else. It is even more
powerful when you find yourself thankful for the gifts in your life.
Gratitude is a high-energy, positive vibration of thought.

I.   Write a list of 10 things in your life for which you are
grateful. Think of 5 people for whom you are grateful, and write
their names and a sentence indicating why you are grateful for their
presence in your life.

_____
_____
_____
_____
_____

One of the most difficult challenges for some people is finding the ability to forgive. Reflect on how you feel when you perceive others have wronged you, or ponder how you feel after you've made a mistake or perceived an imperfection in yourself.

II.   Think about how you feel holding on to resentment. Next, ponder the cost of your freedom, when you are caught feeling hard hearted. How do you free yourself? How do you feel when someone forgives you? Read the following sentence, and write a paragraph explaining its wisdom. "Holding resentment is like drinking poison and waiting for the other person to die."

_____

_____

_____

_____

_____

_____

_____

_____

_____

_____

_____

_____

_____

_____

_____

_____

_____

_____

_____

_____

_____

_____

_____

_____

_____

Every individual has his own beliefs when it comes to giving.

III.   What is your belief about giving? How has it served you?
Do you need to modify it? Have you taught your children to give?
How does your family give?

_____

_____

_____

_____

_____

_____

_____

_____

_____

_____

_____

_____

_____

_____

_____

_____

_____

_____

_____

_____

_____

_____

_____

_____

_____

_____

_____

_____

_____

_____

_____

_____

_____

_____

_____

_____

_____

ALEX, RAZ, LARRY AND CHARISMA STEPHEN

Chapter 10

THE LEGACY MODULE

"I want people to remember my persistence and that I never gave up on my
goals and dreams. You must do the same."
~Larry Stephen~

WORKSHEETS

Plant communities in your life and in the world. Leave people with
examples of creating, planting and finding a community. Your sense
of community might not be to help illuminate life for Deaf people,
but only you can search your heart to know what you care about.

I.   Reflect on your legacy. What is it? Describe its positive,
loving seed, remembering that what you can clearly visualize, you can
more easily manifest. How do you wish to see your legacy flourish in
the world?

_____

_____

_____

_____

_____

_____

_____

_____

ALEX, RAZ, LARRY AND CHARISMA STEPHEN

II.   What legacy would you like your children to leave in the world?   Do you communicate with your children to know their dreams and goals?   If no, why not?   There is no better time to find out than now.

_____

_____

_____

_____

_____

_____

_____

_____

_____

_____

_____

_____

_____

_____

_____

_____

_____

_____

_____

_____

_____

_____

_____

_____

_____

_____

_____

_____

_____

_____

_____

_____

_____

_____

The authors of this accompaniment wish you peace, love, wealth and health. Please contact us via the information on the LINKS page, if you should desire to contact us for speaking engagements and conferences. Peace and Blessings.

III.   How has the reading of this book and the completion of the writing assignments impacted your life? Would you recommend this book to a friend? Why or why not? Please bless the authors by writing a review on Amazon or on other online, book-selling sites.

_____
_____
_____
_____
_____
_____
_____
_____
_____
_____
_____
_____
_____
_____
_____
_____
_____
_____
_____
_____
_____
_____
_____
_____
_____
_____
_____
_____
_____
_____
_____
_____
_____

ALEX, RAZ, LARRY AND CHARISMA STEPHEN

CONCLUSION

It has been our humble pleasure and sincere delight to have shared our journey and unique life experiences with you in our book, **Courage in our Hearts™ ~ A Family's Love Story**. If you have yet to read it, we hope that you will read it very soon. As you move through the modules and the composition exercises in this accompaniment to **Courage in our Hearts™**, we pray you have been empowered in some way to discover your inner treasure.

Please continue to reflect on and complete the exercises thoughtfully. We believe you will experience unimaginable miracles.

If you are interested in furthering your quest for a better lifestyle, you can download our FREE personal development products at www.pdpowerpack.com.

In addition, receive a FREE strategy session with Alex Stephen, if you are interested in procuring the services of a transformational/lifestyle coach. For more information, please visit www.meetwithalex.com.

ABOUT THE AUTHORS

ALEX STEPHEN

Alex is an author, speaker and Transformation/Lifestyle Coach. Passionate about transforming lives around the globe by helping people identify and live their life's purpose, he uses his own life as an example of how to live your purpose and automatically create a legacy for your loved ones. A Howard University honor graduate and a Certified Public Accountant (CPA), Alex built a distinguished, 20-year career in business finance where he held titles such as Corporate Loan Officer and Vice President/Director.

RAZ STEPHEN

Raz is an author, speaker and Transformation/Lifestyle Coach, who joins her husband in touching lives and changing destinies of those who hear and read the awe-inspiring story of their life journey. The dynamic mother, grandmother and business woman holds a managerial position in a major software company. Raz is a Howard University honor graduate with a Bachelor's in Math and Computer Science and a Master's in Computer Science.

LARRY STEPHEN

Larry is an author and a graduate of California State University, Northridge. He holds a Bachelor of Arts in Geography and a Master's in Deaf Education from McDaniel College in Maryland. A renowned athlete, he was a Division I and USA Deaf Olympic soccer player. Additionally, he is a founder and leader in various Deaf organizations, as well as an Associate Professor in ASL at a college in MA.

CHARISMA STEPHEN

Charisma is an author and an honor graduate of Northeastern University, Boston. She holds a Bachelor's in Music Industry and Business. A project coordinator for the state of MA, Charisma is fluent in American Sign Language (ASL). She is living her dreams and following her passion in the music industry. And yes, she lives up to her name...Charisma.

LINKS AND CONTACTS

The Stephen Family can be reached via the following links and contacts:

http://www.LifeTransformingTreasures.com
www.LifeTransformingTreasures.com

Free Personal Development Products   www.pdpowerpack.com
www.NextLevelRiches.com ~ A home-study training system with video, audio, PDF and worksheets

Free Strategy Session   www.meetwithalex.com

http://www.LTT7.com/guide
www.LTT7.com/guide~ Transformation Coaching on a one-on-one basis

info@LTT7.com

www.alexstephen.com ~ Speaking/Coaching

Mail to:

Life Transforming Treasures Corporation
P.O. Box 157
Marlboro, MA 01752
USA

www.ingramcontent.com/pod-product-compliance
Lightning Source LLC
Chambersburg PA
CBHW062030040426
42447CB00010B/2221